Don't Ever Be Too Old

Leah Johnston-Rowbotham

outskirts
press

DEDICATION

for my sister, ***Peggy***,
our family prayer whisperer
who takes wonderous care of us all…

Table of Contents

Acknowledgements:

to my husband who loved me through all of our journeys…the good and the not so good…to my children and to those that they love…to my grandchildren who I love with unconditional positive regard… to my family and friends who never quite got my writing but encouraged me anyway…to my family and friends who got my writing and told me to stay at it…to laura boss who told me way back in the 1990's to "keep writing…." to that faithful group of poets in laura's classes who I have written with for well over 20 years or so… to marian calabro who always edited without criticism or judgment…to my thursday night family and to my fellow café poets…to *vista publishing* who put out my first book in 1998…to my STOOP family and senior poets who amaze me and support me through this ever changing and challenging time in our lives…ljr

Don't ever be too old...

INTRODUCTION:

This is a book of my thoughts...my thoughts that I have written without filter. Some are one line long. Some are much longer. None are longer than one page. As I get precariously close to old in this ever changing and precariously hazardous world I am more acutely aware of how much I want to give to my friends, family, children and grandchildren. They are seldom in need of my direct advice or opinions; nor do they really want it. I am not really in a physical or financial position to carry or relieve some of their burdens; but I suppose that somewhere along the line some of them, every once in a while, might appreciate one of my thoughts. Not lectures. Not run-on-sentences. Not novels. Just a few thoughts that I have not filtered. I invite you to come inside these pages and read in bits and pieces. My hope is that you might want to hold onto one or two of them, even if just for a moment.

I say thank you to each and every one of you who
have brightly quilted your way through my life.
You have been a treasured gift. I thank you for that
and ask that you not ever be too old…

to love theater buttered popcorn
and
hot flaky biscuits
and
the smell of church on easter
and
the feel of warm towels fresh from the dryer
and
and the solemnity of the high holy days
and
honeyed surgared tea
and
the tingly pitchy sound
of
a child's first song.

Don't dismiss your daydreams;

they can allow the grandest of your imagination
to present itself to you in technicolor...

At all ages

one must still seek out prophets
to guide the children of our childrens' children.

Sometimes the littlest

of a moment
the littlest of a thought
a smidgeon of a feeling
has a need to be shared…

a raindrop in perfect form upon a child's fingertip
a snowflake on a twig
a smile on a sleeping face
a sigh meant to be heard.

The sun was out today

and warmed me
through the glass
of the university library windows
in a deceptive manner
as the thermometer read 17 degrees;
but sometimes maybe such deception
is not deception
but a gifted illusion to soothe me
in the dull greyness of winter.

Being old

does not necessarily make one obsolete.

Some days are really hard

they demand a decision.
does one drag through them?
does one crawl back under the quilt?
or does one step into
cotton candy pink embroidered cowgirl boots
with the most ferocious of courage
and claim the day and own it......just own it....

To be significant

is to matter …
even when you might not think that you do.

It was 32 degrees today

bright out but still cold
I do not like cold
spring should come sooner
it was only February
I already dressed in black tights, black shirt, black
boots
I grabbed in to the back of my closet
found a pair of bright lime colored balloon style
pants
and pulled them on.
Yes, I thought. That should do it.
spring will come.

I will try

to celebrate the color of a purple crocus
in the greyest
of a late winter day.

I find it takes

much more energy and time
to try and get rid of all the extemporaneous
thoughts
flitting through my head
than it takes to let them just float on through
in their own good time.

Did you ever notice that

sometimes five minutes can seem like an eternity
while at other times
whole pieces of our journey can be gone
before we think to leave footprints behind?

There are times

when trying to keep one's mind focused on the
issue at hand
is as impossible
as expecting puppies in a crate to sit still.
So, I do not try for awhile...
sometimes for a long while.

Many times

the first step can be quite wobbly but if we don't
take it
we will never get to the next one.

There is

a yeasty, intoxicating smell about freshly baked
italian bread
that dares one to say
"No, Thank You."
when passed to you along with the bowl of
steaming
golden pasta covered in Sunday's marinara gravy.

If it is true

that an average woman
outlives an average man by seven years I wonder
what I will do
with the twenty-five hundred or so extra days????

If today

is a sad, hard, hurting, lonely kind of day
then I do not need to make believe
that it is anything other than that
at least just for today.

That story

about the loaves and the fishes
tells me that if I feed them they will come
but it does not tell me
that they will stay and listen.

Sometimes

I need to forgive
not forget…not learn to live with…
not tolerate…not put up with…
just forgive.

Manners are always

felt by others; so, I really do try to be polite.

Someone once told me

to look for the commonality
to acknowledge that which makes us more alike
than different
and I think that I will try that more often.

I've been talking

to so many dead people lately
that my children worry about me
but I think that it is OK
the talking, that is, not the worrying.

If you see

buds on a tree today
hold on to the promise.

Cherish the space

of early summer before air conditioning
clogs windows and creates a vacuum
where life outside the white linen of curtain
is numbed and shrouded.

I wonder

If I'll die
I know others who have died
I've mourned others who have died
but I wonder if I will die
I don't think so.

My Nana once said

that the answer was there
even if I couldn't see it right away
without risking my way through the fog.

I am not in their head.

I am not in their head.
I am not in their head. I am not in their head.
SO:
how could I possibly know
what they are thinking
unless I *ask them...*

Guess what?

I really, really need to honestly and thoroughly
know that
I am not always right…
[even when I am positively, absolutely sure that I
am right].

I watched

as she rocked her baby with a gentle rhythm
older than time itself.

I think

that most people like to be treated
like they are special; like they are important;
like they are of value; but most of all
I think that most people
just like to be treated like they matter;
like they really, really matter.

If one

possesses the "nightingale" gene
and
practices care giving
then one must continually
nurture one's own self
so that one does not run out of the caring
that one gives.

I have

enough food
I have shoes on my feet
I have heat when it's cold
and a porch and shade tree in the summer
I have some watermelon
and a library card.
I guess I'm set for life…

Life will often demand

that we separate
our wants from our needs
in order to lead a "grown-up" life.
I suppose that is true; but I say
don't ever forget to leave in some of the wants
like red boots and your motorcycle
and a Queens' concert and llamas and lambs
and a real live honest to god smell
of the pine Christmas tree .

Effort

is often of great value unto itself.

If I ever get the chance

to personally speak with Leonardo about his portrait of Mona Lisa, I might be brazen enough to ask him why he picked the model he did. Think about it for just a minute. Even though it has held up as an awesome and amazing piece of art, don't you think that if he had chosen as his model someone like Oprah, or Bernadette Peters, or Sofia Vergara that there might have been an added spark to his work.

Just a thought…

If I cannot

walk on water, why do I think

I can control another person?

I will find

the sun today
I might have to look harder than yesterday
I might have to look longer than yesterday
but I will do it
I will find the sun today.

Every night

remind a child
to capture a moon beam
and toss it high
and watch the sky
embrace its glow
and sprinkle it back
as starlight.

If I can remember that

I own everything that comes out of my mouth
I just might say less.

An old man once told me

that our town had stopped planting
flowering pear trees
because their branches did not bend
with cold and ice and snow and wind
they just broke off
I guess that tells me something about the need
at times
to be flexible.

Today

I'd like to stay home and
take pictures of wintered sun and
write 10 poems of epic unimportance and
make mixes of music as old as Joan Baez and
so, I shall.

I know that you loved me

really really loved me
do you know how I know
because I leaned into your warmth
when you were near
and
I lean into your warmth
even when you are not near.

There is definitely

something to be said
for honing the gift of resilience.
It helps one get up
over and over and over again…

I remember someone

telling me once that the word
assessment comes from the latin word sedere
which loosely translated means to sit beside
and I thought what a nice way to assess someone,
sitting beside them instead of above them.

I am humbled,

challenged, fearful, mindful, inspired,
thoughtful, and usually laughing whenever
I remember the last time
I thought that I could walk on water.

I do chuckle

when I think that someone else thinks
that they have the power to change me
and yet I do not always remember to chuckle
when I think that I have the power
to change someone else.

It was

not the child
who spoke out of turn
but rather the adult
who did not know when her turn was up.

Every woman

should get to wear a tiara for at least a day
or maybe a day and a night
or maybe a week or so
or a year or two
or maybe just whenever she feels like it…

The oldest brother said

his mother basted the ham with honey
the next brother said she basted it
with a mixture of honey and brown sugar
and the next brother said she basted it
with a mixture of mustard, marmalade, and
brown sugar
and one sister said she didn't know
and another sister said
who cares?

It can take a certain arrogance

to glance at wrinkles in the mirror
with ownership.

6 pm

I wonder about so many feelings,
so many thoughts,
so many need-to-tell stories at the end of a day
and I wonder if
we leave each other enough time to tell them.

This morning

say an extra thank you
whisper an extra I love you
remember a warm thought and hold it tight
and I think this afternoon will be good…

Those three kings

did a lot of traveling
led only by a star on a trip
dictated only on faith in the mere goodness
of another human being.
sound about right to you?

If you are cold

do you reach for a coat?
if you are thirsty,
do you reach for a glass of water?
If you are in need of comfort
do you seek comfort?

Quite often

I forget to use today's energy
Just for today.

It can "occasionally"

be quite difficult
to not jump to one's own conclusion
prior
to the end of another's explanation.

One might try to remember

to wear her red silk teddy
under her grey tailored business suit
on the day she moves into the corner office.

She blessed herself

as if she believed that a god was there
and that he heard her when she beckoned him
and asked for grace.

I will try harder

to not talk out loud to myself
when I am in a crowded elevator.

I looked around

at the other people
in the waiting room this morning
and was surprised
that I was so much younger than
everyone else and then I was even more surprised
when I realized that I wasn't.

As I looked up

at my father's smile of vacant sweetness
I re-wrapped the scarf around his neck
in much the same way
as he had done so many times for me.

Sometimes I am

just so over programmed to accomplish
that I miss the doves' cooing
or the child's giggle
or the crackle in the air before a storm
or the heavy sigh of another,
or the whispered prayer
I did not know I said.

All of us own

some bits and pieces of "flightsomeness"
and dramatic ways
and we all tinker with a love
for outrageous polished
rust colored satin edged crinolines
worn underneath ankle length denim skirts
with cowboy boots;
but only a few of us
openly declare ownership of such whims.

Love the sheer dichotomy

of vanilla ice cream
swirled through with black raspberries
and ebony skin on top of alabaster skin
and a nurse's clog
beside a skinny spiky heeled strappy sandal
and maybe not love so much the sheer dichotomy of
the blazing contrast
between true really-believe-it kind of faith and
the agonizing-trying-hoping-wanting-it
to be there kind of faith.

If there really is a St. Peter

standing guard at the golden gates of heaven
as I was told when I was a kid
and that as a grown up
while living down here on earth
I could never afford to live in a wealthy gated
community
does that mean
that I will never be allowed through
the golden gates
of St. Peter's heavenly gates when I die?

It's been a long time

since he left me; but I am still here
and still shudder a little and sometimes
a little more than a little
whenever I am caught in that moment
when I again re-remember
vividly re-remember that he is not here.

Sometimes all I need

Is someone to tell me to give it up
sometimes all I need
is someone to tell me to get on with it
sometimes all I need
is someone to tell me to let it go
sometimes all I need
is for someone to listen, just listen
and not tell me what to do.

Someone told me once

that everyday was a day that their lord had made
and I asked her
why he always crowded so much into it.

Late on Sunday afternoons

their dad would take them
across the street to the parking lot
to search for pennies
and other such "valuables" found on the ground
between sandy patches of grass and blacktop.
They took this task with great seriousness
and were tenacious
in their search
even when they were old enough to know
that it was a lot of work for usual slim pickins
but that mattered little to them.
It was not about the found booty.
It was all about the hunt,
the companionship, the camaraderie of it all.
It was about the time with their dad and siblings

and hope.
It was about believing.
It was about knowing
that there was always something
around the corner,
something good.
There is always another penny on the ground.
You just have to do the search.

So what

If the vanilla latte was cold by the time,
I got to drink it.
Give it up, I say.   That's why someone
out there in the almighty universe
created microwaves.

only the smoothest

of ocean smoothed stone
the smallest mahogany acorn
and a little bit mushy hershey kiss
were allowed inside the denim pocket
buttoned ever so carefully
with the pink laced flap
by the four-year-old
and I wonder....
when one's ideas of genuine value change.

I am ok

with opinions
I am ok with suggestions
I am ok with disagreements
I am ok with critique
I am not ok with judgment calls.

Every once in a very great while

allow yourself to indulge in a moment of fantasy
and be surrounded in a quiet hush
only broken
by the swishing of angel wings
and the rustling of satin gowns
as you are gently lifted
above the hypervigilance of the everyday
as a calming aura above and within
completes who you are
in a peace dappled moment of utter lightness.

I am capable

of a larger, stronger, more diverse network
then I ever thought possible
by merely being open
to the possibility of one.

I am really glad

that I have learned to own up to when I am
wrong
and to say that I am sorry
without the words sticking in my throat
wow
but doesn't that make life a little lighter.

I thought about my friend Robin

who was the first chair violinist for the NYC
Ballet,
and only dressed in the most conservative
of long black dresses
and ballet flats both at work and not at work.
Her glass frames were black,
and her lenses were thick.
She seldom wore makeup.
She was getting married tomorrow
and was entering into the gated city
reigning atop a bejeweled,
brocaded draped satin veiled elephant
of immense size
as she herself was adorned
in the finest and richest of design
partially hidden by heavy gold
and brilliant diamonds.
Who would have thought to judge a book
by only one of its many covers?????

Intensity

can be a wonderous and productive state
as long as one remembers that the consistent use
of so much
of one's raw energy demands the consistent
nurturing and replacement of said energy or else
KERPLUNK!

If one were a wizard

instead of just human
I do not think that it would be quite as
impressive
when one works really, really hard
to do the right thing...
as when a human
works really, really hard
to do the right thing...
don't you think?

Every once in awhile I need

to sit still
stay quiet
and
pay attention
pay attention to just myself.

Don't ever underestimate

the power of kayaks and coconuts and elephants
and spring break
and brass rings and steak with cheese
and the tiniest of sweet green grapes
and pencils and quilts and pink kangaroos
and the easiness of his hand
on your lower back
as you walk into the restaurant.

I have

a walking stick that steadies the sidewalk for
me and a hot tub that warms the winter and a
longing to dismiss loneliness and a window that
imagines the scent of the sea and I had two doves
that cooed in my city yard and a mama who
walks through dementia and a warmth that carries
through fall and teases the frigidness of nakedness
and I have some children who have some children
and I have a child who does not have his child yet
and I have the gift of the "shannikee", the gift of
tales and storied lore, the sacred gift, the cherished
gift, the gift passed down from an Irish Traveller.

Spend some time this week

writing the harder list. Not the
"what-I-have-to-do-list"
or "what-I-should-do-list" but the
"what-I-want-to-do-list"
the really, really important list that mentions
playing an Irish drum
that carries a jig as easily as a funeral march,
or buying
two frozen coffees in one day, or singing James
Arthur's song
over and over again about not letting me go even
when we are
ghosts or sailing the Mediterranean or eating
peanut butter
crackers and russian caviar with irish vodka.   All
your choice.
blessedly, delightfully, freely your own, not
pressured, no quilt
your kind of choice.

I think that anger

does not have to be an unending verb;
it can be a noun
with a beginning and an end
if we want it to be.

I will not be afraid

just for this week or maybe just for today or
maybe just for this morning or maybe just for this
one hour or maybe for the next ten minutes or
maybe just for this moment in time
to make a mistake.
No; I won't let my life be governed by the fear of
making mistakes.

Sometime today

listen to the humming song from Madam
Butterfly
and hold it tight
for times when you forget to seek soothing.

I must remember that

bills are a part of my life
but that they are not my life.

I really cannot

walk in another person's shoes.
They just don't fit right.

I hope

that my children and their children
remember that I really liked them.

I love the Atlantic Ocean

better than the Pacific Ocean
and the Caribbean better than the Atlantic
and the Mediterranean better than the Caribbean
and I know that it is alright to like somethings
and some people
better than others and that there is no need to
psychoanalyze
all of that.

There is great worth

in run on sentences that free the structure that
tend to end a thought before a conclusion and
then again cannot that lead to rambling in circles
back to the beginning without conclusion which
might encourage one to try it every once in awhile
without a measured word or thought in order to
feel the freedom that breathes a little faster as it
allows the sometimes unstated integral parts to
fall into place.

I love

the smell of sun-kissed skin and baby's breath
and cinnamon and fresh cut pineapple and
evergreen
and I love them all the best when I can close my
eyes
and call them up as needed.

I will try to acknowledge

the sacredness of the everyday.

Sometimes it is alright

to just feel really, really sad...

You are probably

in the right relationship if you feel better about
yourself when you are in it then you did
when you were not in it.

Sometimes ADHD

can be a gift when I need to be attentive to several
underlying currents occurring at the same time
as long as I can manage to not jumble them all
together
at the same time.

I have found that

I am not comfortable with conversating with someone while they are "multi- conversatating". I tend to conversate better in a one-to-one kind of way. I even prefer to look at people when we talk with one another. I don't know. It just seems to work better for me.

If Lucy

still tends to pull the football out of your reach
right before you get to kick it; try to remember
that it happens to a lot more people than you
think. Just be a little more hypervigilant along
your way in life and still carry an almighty,
nourishing, ever empowering belief that every
single human being holds within them a kernel of
goodness. I think that it is this belief that helps
me to sleep at night.

Birthdays are for...

giggling...thinking...planning...playing...
sailing...loving...
dancing...crying [a little] ...
looking back... looking ahead...celebrating...
quiet time...
giving back...forgiving...saying please...
singing...
napping...indulging...wondering...
running...planting...saying thank you...
looking around...
hugging a lot...hugging a whole, whole lot...
creating...critiquing...imagining...
being in the moment....
and solemnly embracing the sacred awe
of having been born.

It's true, don't you know,

that all beginnings and endings are covered
in the bitter sweetness of it all.

Once upon a time

we were left one another to take care of…

I might need to

darken the backdrop
to see the light.

I do not believe

that great insight
comes out of chaos and noise
but rather out of silence
even if that silence
is carved out of the chaos of one's life
long enough for one
to detach, think, and listen.

Marriage is

wondrous, audacious, engaging, grueling,
exhausting,
overwhelming, compelling, demanding,
comforting, binding,
freeing, outrageous, generous, getting angry,
laughing, selfless,
all-encompassing, fun, getting over the anger,
catalytic, selfish,
time consuming, slow dancing outside the
laundry room,
protective, inspiring, thrilling, being in the right
place,
with the right person,
and always knowing that you are cherished
even on a bad day.

May I never underestimate

kayaks and coconuts and elephants
and spring break
and brass rings and steak with cheese
and the tiniest of sweet green grapes
and pencils and quilts and pink kangaroos
and the easiness of his hand
on my lower back as we walk into the restaurant.

One who is audacious

can be thought to be
one who is contemptuous or impudent
or one who is simply courageous enough to color
outside of *the lines.*

take time today

just a moment or two
not too long
to remember that there is still
an immense amount of awe in our lives
if only we take that moment
just a very little moment
to savor it.

Try being brave for just one day

and hold your courage right out loud
and ban all cell phones, i pads, i pods, computers,
and any other such devices
from breakfast, lunch, and dinner tables,
and beaches and lake fronts and bedrooms,
and any and all such places
that may better serve all involved
with one on one respectful attention
such as you yourself deserve
without the constant distraction from said
devices
on a consistent and constant basis.

We all have little pieces

of happy moments
like when we find the perfect shade of blush
or the train is on time,
or you grabbed your favorite wine glass
just before it hit the marble counter top and
shattered
or when for a fleeting, unexpected second
you feel overwhelmed
with the deeply invasive knowledge of his love.

When it is hard to be quiet,

it is usually a pretty good time
for me to do so.

Sometimes I say,

I would never interfere,
just give suggestions.
Maybe I need to think a little more
about that one.

I sometimes forget

to consider the source
not whether or not I like the source.

Taking a risk

does not necessarily imply
acting impulsively.

I think that it is OK

to sometimes feel old;
Just not OK to always think old.

I know that she doesn't like me.

but is it still OK to like her?

Did you ever wonder

how it is possible for every single one of us
to have a very different, very individual,
very singularly identifiable voice
that is very uniquely our own
and able to be identified and heard
as our voice
in this very noisy world?

Go and follow the smile

you felt as a child
on the first morning of summer.

I really,

really, really, really do not have a lot of patience;
so, a lot of times in my life
I just have to make believe that I do...

I like ocean waves,

I like sea waves, I like bay waves,
I like lake and river waves;
but I do not like the waves of grief.
They come out of nowhere.
They suck you in to the aloneness of a grey world.
They devastate, deplete, and weary the very
weariness of you.
So, you try to remember
that they do not last forever.
Yes. They come back.
But they do not last forever.

He always told me that

you already parented them once.
You don't get to do it again.

Favorite part of my life?

the middle part....
being married to my best friend
and raising our kids together.
Yes, that was my very, very favorite part.

I wonder

if there is really a special time for life review
or if we always do it and just don't always
learn from it.

When I start to panic

too often about having late onset dementia
because of my forgetting some things,
I remind myself that I have at least 70 some years
of stored memory
to go through before it is all gone.
I do not believe I will live until I am 140.
I guess that gives me less reason to panic about
forgetting where my
glasses are or that I left a bag of groceries in the
car yesterday.

Their Pop

took a pile of gravely, sandy
not-so-rich downtown kind of dirt
and put it in the bottom
of an old wooden packing crate
and grew a delectable, shiny pepper
right in the middle of his tiny front yard
in the middle of downtown.
yup, he did that;
so just think about what you can do
if you want to......

CPSIA information can be obtained
at www.ICGtesting.com
Printed in the USA
BVHW040926280621
610635BV00018BA/423